A SPONSOR WHO PRAYS

A Journal to Guide You in Praying
For Your Confirmand

Katie Warner

If the lungs of prayer and of the Word of God do not nourish the breath of spiritual life, we risk suffocating in the midst of a thousand daily cares. Prayer is the breath of the soul and of life.

-Pope Benedict XVI-

Dear sponsor,

Perhaps there is no greater gift we can give our confirmandi than the gift of our prayers. As sponsors we can help the life of grace flourish within their souls in praying fervently for them, aiding God in transforming them into the people He desires them to be.

As sponsors, we have the beautiful responsibility to provide spiritual guardianship to our confirmandi over the course of their lives. We should take this duty very seriously, becoming active examples of Christian discipleship for them to observe and follow.

But one of the greatest things we can do to aid in the effort of guiding our confirmandi toward a vibrant, life-long faith is to pray for them.

Your confirmand obviously admire the faith that you have, and hopes that you will be a witness to God's love and His work in his or her life. Don't allow your confirmand's baptism days to be the only day that you fulfill that special evangelistic role in his or her life.

Allow this simple prayer guide and journal to give you the motivation and tools you need to make praying for your confirmand a priority this year—and always.

May Jesus remain ever close to your confirmand's heart, may our Blessed Mother always keep him/her or under Her mantle, may St. Joseph be your confirmand's heavenly guardian, and may the guardian angels always protect him/her.

Katie Warner
KatieWarner.com

How to Use **A Sponsor Who Prays**

1. Once a week (put it on your schedule!), sit down with this journal and put yourself in God's presence. **Sit in silence** for a few minutes, allowing your other daily duties to take a back seat to the beautiful work of praying for your confirmand(i) for a moment.

2. **Read the special intention for the week**, with accompanying Scripture, quote, or reflection, and pray for that special virtue or intention listed to grow, with God's grace, in your confirmand(i).

3. Write down and pray about any additional, **specific intentions** that are on the forefront of your mind related to your confirmand(i). (Examples: a problem they are having at school, a big decision they must make, an emotional struggle they are going through, a health issue, a challenging relationship in their life, etc.) This is a great opportunity to connect with your confirmand on a regular basis through text, email, phone, or in person to learn what's going on in your confirmand's life.

4. **Continue to pray** for the week's special and specific intentions each day that week. Refer to your journal/guide as needed. When praying the prayer provided on the page, substitute your confirmand(i)'s name(s) to make the prayers more personal.

5. At the end of the week, **offer a spiritual bouquet** for your confirmand(i) by writing down any gifts of prayer you offered that week for their specific intentions and the special intention provided. (Consider planning ahead by writing these down and then checking off as completed.) Some examples of gifts of prayer include:
    *   Masses
    *   Rosaries, Chaplets, and Novenas
    *   Individual prayers: Our Father, Hail Mary, Glory Be, the Memorare, Angelus, or the Prayer to the Holy Family (on next page)
    *   Daily sufferings and frustrations
    *   Daily successes and joys
    *   Fasting

This prayer guide can certainly remain a private journal. However, if you choose to gift this to one of your confirmandi at any point in time, the collection of these weekly bouquets will no doubt be an amazing offering of love to him or her, allowing your confirmand to see how your unceasing prayers are one of the most important ways you provide spiritual support as a sponsor. There is room for an optional note on the following page.

No greater joy can I have than this, to hear that my children follow the truth.

-3 John 1:4-

PRAYER FOR MY CONFIRMAND

Jesus, I come to you with a humble heart
And pray for someone dear to my heart –
my confirmand who was entrusted to me.

Give me the grace to encourage my confirmand in the faith,
to pray for him/her fervently,
so that my confirmand may grow closer to You.
Help me to be an example of a devoted follower of yours.

I pray that my confirmand will
first and foremost know your love,
that he/she will always walk in your ways,
grow in virtue,
and foster an ever-deepening relationship with You.

I pray for my confirmand to have health of soul, mind, and body,
to have strong friendships and family ties,
and to stay close to your Church.

I pray that my confirmand may always find grace and strength in the sacraments,
that he/she may be open to Your plan for his/her life and vocation,
and that my confirmand will someday experience eternal happiness with you in heaven as one of your saints.

Jesus, through the intercession of Mother Mary and St. Joseph,
hear my prayer and richly bless my confirmand.

Amen.

PURITY

Blessed are the pure in heart, for they shall see God.
–Matthew 5:8

We must be pure. I do not speak merely of the purity of the senses.
We must observe great purity in our will, in our intentions, in all our
actions. - Saint Peter Julian Eymard

THIS WEEK'S **SPECIFIC INTENTIONS** FOR MY CONFIRMAND(I):

Lord, I ask you to hear these special intentions, together with my
petition for my confirmand's ongoing growth in purity, and I
humbly offer you the spiritual bouquet below. Please bind these
prayers together with your grace, and allow my confirmand to
become a holy model of purity—purity of heart, of mind, and of
body—in his/her family and in our world, which is so in need of sons
and daughters of God who are filled with purity.

MY **SPIRITUAL BOUQUET** FOR THIS WEEK:

FAITH

For truly, I say to you, if you have faith as a grain of mustard seed, you will say to this mountain, `Move from here to there,' and it will move; and nothing will be impossible to you. -Matthew 17:20

Faith is to believe what you do not see; the reward of this faith is to see what you believe. - Saint Augustine

THIS WEEK'S **SPECIFIC INTENTIONS** FOR MY CONFIRMAND(I):

Lord, I ask you to hear these special intentions, together with my petition for my confirmand's ongoing growth in faith, and I humbly offer you the spiritual bouquet below. Please bind these prayers together with your grace, and allow my confirmand to have a faith that stands strong amidst our culture's attempts to weaken it. Help him/her love to learn about the faith, so that through constantly expanding his/her knowledge of you, my confirmand can grow in love of you, too.

MY **SPIRITUAL BOUQUET** FOR THIS WEEK:

PEACE

And the peace of God, which passes all understanding, will keep your hearts and your minds in Christ Jesus.
–Philippians 4:7

Never be in a hurry; do everything quietly and in a calm spirit. Do not lose your inner peace for anything whatsoever, even if your whole world seems upset. - Saint Francis de Sales

THIS WEEK'S **SPECIFIC INTENTIONS** FOR MY CONFIRMAND(I):

Lord, I pray for these special intentions and for my confirmand to grow in peace, and I humbly offer you the spiritual bouquet below. With the help of your grace, allow my confirmand to live a life characterized by peace and not anxiety, handing over worries to You. Help me to teach him/her how to see areas in their life where his/her peace of heart is being threatened, and then have the courage to make changes to restore your life-sustaining peace.

MY **SPIRITUAL BOUQUET** FOR THIS WEEK:

HUMILITY

Do nothing from selfishness or conceit, but in humility count others better than yourselves. –Philippians 2:3

Someone once asked St. Bernard of Clairvaux what the three most important virtues are. He famously replied, "Humility, humility and humility."

THIS WEEK'S **SPECIFIC INTENTIONS** FOR MY CONFIRMAND(I):

Lord, I pray for these special intentions and for my confirmand to grow in humility, and I offer you the spiritual bouquet below. With the help of your grace, allow my confirmand to become a truly humble individual, who does not seek acclaim or earthly glory, but faithfulness to you. Help him/her encourage others, rather than foster a spirit of pride or competitiveness. Give my confirmand the humility to recognize his/her weaknesses, and the grace to improve upon them.

MY **SPIRITUAL BOUQUET** FOR THIS WEEK:

GRATITUDE

＞＞－－－＜＜

Give thanks in all circumstances; for this is the will of God in Christ
Jesus for you. –1 Thessalonians 5:18

No duty is more urgent than that of returning thanks.
- St. Ambrose

THIS WEEK'S **SPECIFIC INTENTIONS** FOR MY CONFIRMAND(I):

Lord, I pray for these special intentions and for my confirmand to
become more grateful, and I offer you the spiritual bouquet
below. With the help of your grace, help him/her grow ever more
appreciative of the blessings and gifts you have given. Help me
teach him/her how to always offer prayers and words of
thanksgiving to you, and to express gratitude to others frequently. I
pray that my confirmand counts his/her blessings more than
complaints.

MY **SPIRITUAL BOUQUET** FOR THIS WEEK:

PATIENCE

Be still before the LORD, and wait patiently for him.
–Psalm 37:7

Patience attains all that it strives for. He who has God finds he lacks nothing: God alone suffices. - St. Teresa of Avila

THIS WEEK'S **SPECIFIC INTENTIONS** FOR MY CONFIRMAND(I):

Lord, I pray for these special intentions and for my confirmand to grow in patience, and I offer you the spiritual bouquet below. With the help of your grace, help him/her to become patient in waiting for both small things (like graduation or a vacation) and big things (like their future vocation). Help him/her learn how to extend greater patience to others and learn how to be patient with him/herself and with his/her faults. Give my confirmand the patience that turns sinners into saints.

MY **SPIRITUAL BOUQUET** FOR THIS WEEK:

HOPE

For I know the plans I have for you, says the LORD, plans for welfare
and not for evil, to give you a future and a hope.
–Jeremiah 29:11

Consult not your fears but your hopes and your dreams. Think not
about your frustrations, but about your unfulfilled potential.
Concern yourself not with what you tried and failed in, but with
what it is still possible for you to do.
–Pope John XXIII

THIS WEEK'S **SPECIFIC INTENTIONS** FOR MY CONFIRMAND(I):

Lord, I pray for these special intentions and for my confirmand to
always have hope, and I offer you this spiritual bouquet. With the
help of your grace, allow him/her to hold onto the hope that gives
meaning to life and strength to push forward in adversity. Help
him/her always embrace hope for his/her *heavenly* destination
that answers the burning desire of the heart for happiness.

MY **SPIRITUAL BOUQUET** FOR THIS WEEK:

No greater joy can I have than this, to hear that my children follow the truth.

-3 John 1:4

PRUDENCE

>>————«<

"I, wisdom, dwell in prudence." –Proverbs 8:12

Blessed the one...who is not anxious to speak, but who reflects prudently on what he is to say and the manner in which he is to reply. –St. Francis of Assisi

THIS WEEK'S **SPECIFIC INTENTIONS** FOR MY CONFIRMAND(I):

Lord, I pray for these special intentions and for my confirmand to become more prudent, and I offer you the spiritual bouquet below. With the help of your grace, I pray that my confirmand learn to apply reason and practical wisdom to everyday decisions and actions—big or small—seeking counsel as needed, using good judgment, and being decisive when he/she knows the right direction in which to move.

MY **SPIRITUAL BOUQUET** FOR THIS WEEK:

JUSTICE

When justice is done, it is a joy to the righteous, but dismay to evildoers. –Proverbs 21:15

The source of justice is not vengeance but charity.
-Saint Bridget of Sweden

THIS WEEK'S **SPECIFIC INTENTIONS** FOR MY CONFIRMAND(I):

Lord, I pray for these special intentions and for my confirmand to become more just, and I offer you the spiritual bouquet below. With the help of your grace, allow my confirmand to always work to maintain and restore justice in the world around him/her—both in and outside the home. Strengthen his/her will to remain firm in giving what is owed to God (like worship) and to others (like the right to life).

MY **SPIRITUAL BOUQUET** FOR THIS WEEK:

TEMPERANCE

Do not follow your base desires, but restrain your appetites.
–Sirach 18:30

Also, temper all your works with moderation, that is to say, all
your abstinence, your fasting, your vigils, and your prayers,
for temperance sustains your body and soul with the proper
measure, lest they fail. –Saint Hildegard

THIS WEEK'S **SPECIFIC INTENTIONS** FOR MY CONFIRMAND(I):

Lord, I pray for these special intentions and for my confirmand to
practice temperance, and I offer you the spiritual bouquet below.
With the help of your grace, I pray my confirmand will learn to
moderate the attraction to worldly pleasure, using material things
in a way that is healthy and leads to not fleeting, but lasting
happiness. Help him/her combat the culture's attempts to allure
my confirmand toward instant gratification and excess.

MY **SPIRITUAL BOUQUET** FOR THIS WEEK:

FORTITUDE

The Lord is my strength and my song. –Psalm 118:14

The person with fortitude is one who perseveres in doing what his conscience tells him he ought to do...The strong man will at times suffer, but he stands firm; he may be driven to tears, but he will brush them aside. When difficulties come thick and fast, he does not bend before them. –Saint Josemaria Escrivá

THIS WEEK'S **SPECIFIC INTENTIONS** FOR MY CONFIRMAND(I):

Lord, I pray for these special intentions and for my confirmand to possess the heroic virtue of fortitude, and I offer you the spiritual bouquet below. With the help of your grace, I pray that he/she will always stand firm amidst difficulties and never stray in the effort to pursue the good. When life gets difficult, let him/her run toward you, and not away from you. Help him/her resist temptations and strive to live a moral life.

MY **SPIRITUAL BOUQUET** FOR THIS WEEK:

VOCATION

I therefore, a prisoner for the Lord, beg you to lead a life worthy of the calling to which you have been called.
–Ephesians 4:1

If you are what you should be, then you will set the world on fire.
–Saint Catherine of Siena

THIS WEEK'S **SPECIFIC INTENTIONS** FOR MY CONFIRMAND(I):

Lord, I pray for these special intentions and for my confirmand's vocation, and I offer you the spiritual bouquet below. You know his/her future, and you hold my confirmand in the palm of your hand. May he/she be open to the plan that you have, which will no doubt put his/her gifts to best use, glorify you, and bring the most fulfillment. Above all, help my confirmand to fulfill his/her ultimate vocation to *love*, whether that be in family life or religious life, and let him/her do this vocational work well.

MY **SPIRITUAL BOUQUET** FOR THIS WEEK:

GENEROSITY

In all things I have shown you that by so toiling one must help the weak, remembering the words of the Lord Jesus, how he said, "It is more blessed to give than to receive."
–Acts 20:35

Teach us to give and not to count the cost.
–St. Ignatius of Loyola

THIS WEEK'S **SPECIFIC INTENTIONS** FOR MY CONFIRMAND(I):

Lord, I pray for these special intentions and for my confirmand to grow in generosity, and I offer you the spiritual bouquet below. Help him/her learn to be generous with time, talent, and treasure. With your grace, help him/her see opportunities to be generous at home (for example, by helping siblings with projects or chores) and outside the home (like by volunteering and contributing to charities).

MY **SPIRITUAL BOUQUET** FOR THIS WEEK:

PRAYER

And this is the confidence which we have in him, that if we ask anything according to his will he hears us. –1 John 5:14

Prayer is the place of refuge for every worry, a foundation for cheerfulness, a source of constant happiness, a protection against sadness.
-St. John Chrysostom

THIS WEEK'S **SPECIFIC INTENTIONS** FOR MY CONFIRMAND(I):

Lord, I pray for these special intentions and for my confirmand to have an ever-deepening prayer life. By your grace, I pray that he/she may come to thirst for more time with you in prayer, always seeking a more intimate relationship and conversation with you, and prioritizing time to grow with you in silence, by prayer with Scripture, and by coming to treasure the great many prayers of the Church.

MY **SPIRITUAL BOUQUET** FOR THIS WEEK:

CONFIDENCE

I can do all things in him who strengthens me.
–Philippians 4:13

Jesus, source of my life, sanctify me. Oh my strength, fortify me. My commander, fight for me. –Saint Faustina

THIS WEEK'S **SPECIFIC INTENTIONS** FOR MY CONFIRMAND(I):

Lord, I pray for these special intentions and for my confirmand to grow in confidence as he/she grow in age, and I present you this spiritual bouquet below. Though there are many threats trying to steal one's confidence in self and in you, Lord, help him/her turn to you for strength. Allow my confirmand to exhibit confidence in the abilities and gifts you've given, in a spirit of humility rather than pride. Allow that confidence to create in him/her a healthy independence, but still a firm dependence on you.

MY **SPIRITUAL BOUQUET** FOR THIS WEEK:

CHASTITY

For this is the will of God, your sanctification: that you abstain from unchastity. –1 Thessalonians 4:3

"Chastity is a difficult, long term matter; one must wait patiently for it to bear fruit, for the happiness of loving kindness which it must bring. But at the same time, chastity is the sure way to happiness." –Pope Saint John Paul II

THIS WEEK'S **SPECIFIC INTENTIONS** FOR MY CONFIRMAND(I):

Lord, I pray for these special intentions and for my confirmand to be chaste, leading up to and throughout his/her lifelong vocation. My God, you know that this virtue is attacked ferociously in our culture today. Give my confirmand the resolve to exhibit chastity in dress, in media consumed, and in his/her relationships. Help my confirmand achieve the "successful integration of [his/her] sexuality" which will lead to unity of body and spirit (CCC 2337).

MY **SPIRITUAL BOUQUET** FOR THIS WEEK:

EDUCATION

Keep hold of instruction, do not let go; guard her, for she is your life. –Proverbs 4:13

True education enables us to love life and opens us to the fullness of life. –Pope Francis

THIS WEEK'S **SPECIFIC INTENTIONS** FOR MY CONFIRMAND(I):

Lord, I pray for these special intentions and for my confirmand's ongoing education. By your grace, instill in him/her a love for learning, regardless of age. Help him/her desire to become a life-long student, always increasing knowledge and understanding of the world and of your truth, goodness, and beauty. Give me the wisdom to hand on important truths while he/she is in my presence, and instill in him/her a desire to direct all educational pursuits to your greater glory.

MY **SPIRITUAL BOUQUET** FOR THIS WEEK:

What really matters in life is that
we are loved by Christ
and that we love Him in
return.
In comparison to the love of
Jesus, everything else is
secondary.
And, without the love of Jesus,
everything is useless.

- Pope Saint John Paul II

FRIENDSHIP WITH MARY

[F]or he has regarded the low estate of his handmaiden. For behold, henceforth all generations will call me blessed. –Luke 1:48

The greatest saints, those richest in grace and virtue will be the most assiduous in praying to the most Blessed Virgin, looking up to her as the perfect model to imitate and as a powerful helper to assist them." -Saint Louis de Montfort

THIS WEEK'S **SPECIFIC INTENTIONS** FOR MY CONFIRMAND(I):

Lord, I pray for these special intentions and for my confirmand's relationship with our Blessed Mother. I know that Scripture and the saints demonstrate how having a close relationship with Mary will lead us closer to you. Help my confirmand to call upon her maternal intercession and allow him/her to see Our Lady as a special heavenly Mother, who is there to protect and comfort him/her, and light the way toward you.

MY **SPIRITUAL BOUQUET** FOR THIS WEEK:

HONORING THE LORD'S DAY

Remember the sabbath day, to keep it holy.
Six days you shall labor, and do all your work; but the seventh day
is a sabbath to the LORD your God;...for in six days the LORD
made heaven and earth... and rested the seventh day; therefore
the LORD blessed the sabbath day and hallowed it.
–Exodus 20:8-11

Repose, leisure, peace, belong among the elements of happiness.
If we have not escaped from harried rush, from mad pursuit, from
unrest, from the necessity of care, we are not happy. –Josef Pieper

THIS WEEK'S **SPECIFIC INTENTIONS** FOR MY CONFIRMAND(I):

Lord, I pray for these intentions and for my confirmand to always
honor the Lord's Day throughout his/her life. By your grace and the
observation of the example I set, help him/her to keep Sunday a
day of rest, worship, play, relaxation, and leisure with loved ones.
Our culture tempts us to work on Sundays; let my confirmand
instead protect Sunday with determination.

MY **SPIRITUAL BOUQUET** FOR THIS WEEK:

SACRAMENTAL LIFE

Do this in remembrance of me. –Luke 22:19

Holy communion is the shortest and safest way to Heaven.
–Saint Pius X

So many people see the confessional as a place of defeat, but confession is a place of victory every single time. –Fr. Mike Schmitz

THIS WEEK'S **SPECIFIC INTENTIONS** FOR MY CONFIRMAND(I):

Lord, I pray for these special intentions, and for my confirmand to have a deep devotion to the sacraments, and I humbly offer you this spiritual bouquet. Infuse my confirmand with your sacramental grace, and help him/her develop a habit of receiving the Holy Eucharist and Reconciliation, so he/she can commune with you, be strengthened by you, and come to you for healing. Let your sacraments transform him/her into the person you are calling my confirmand to be.

MY **SPIRITUAL BOUQUET** FOR THIS WEEK:

ZEAL

Never flag in zeal, be aglow with the Spirit, serve the Lord.
–Romans 12:11

Zeal reveals to us all the difference between a world grown merely
secular and old, and the youthfulness of Christian love.
–Anthony Esolen

THIS WEEK'S **SPECIFIC INTENTIONS** FOR MY CONFIRMAND(I):

Lord, I pray for these special intentions, and for my confirmand
never to lack in zeal, and I offer you this spiritual bouquet. Give
him/her a strong, action-oriented desire to advance in the spiritual
life and move in the direction of righteousness. By your grace, give
him/her the diligence to put love into action and to strengthen the
resolution to progress in virtue and sanctity, making his/her spiritual
life a priority, even when other things threaten to monopolize time
or attention.

MY **SPIRITUAL BOUQUET** FOR THIS WEEK:

FAMILY RELATIONSHIPS

Train up a child in the way he should go, and when he is old he will not depart from it. –Proverbs 22:6

Living together is an art, a patient, beautiful, fascinating journey. It does not end once you have won each other's love... Rather, it is precisely there where it begins!
–Pope Francis

THIS WEEK'S **SPECIFIC INTENTIONS** FOR MY CONFIRMAND(I):

Lord, I pray for these special intentions, and for my confirmand's relationships within his/her family, and I offer you this spiritual bouquet. Please allow family ties to be strong, and for peace and harmony to be present among siblings and between parents and children in the home. I pray that within his/her home, my confirmand can be a part of building a foundation of love and enjoyment of one another that lasts into his/her adulthood.

MY **SPIRITUAL BOUQUET** FOR THIS WEEK:

OBEDIENCE

You shall therefore love the LORD your God, and keep his charge,
his statutes, his ordinances, and his commandments always.
–Deuteronomy 11:1

God is more pleased to behold the lowest degree of obedience,
for His sake, than all other good works which you can possibly offer
to Him. -Saint John of the Cross

THIS WEEK'S **SPECIFIC INTENTIONS** FOR MY CONFIRMAND(I):

Lord, I pray for these special intentions, and for my confirmand to
practice obedience, and I offer you this spiritual bouquet. Through
your grace, allow him/her to see obedience as a beautiful virtue,
even when our culture tries to make obedience seem unnecessary
or burdensome. Help cultivate in him/her a desire to be obedient
to God and His will and laws, obedient to His Church, and
obedient to parents and sponsors, as well as to authority figures
who are deserving of obedience.

MY **SPIRITUAL BOUQUET** FOR THIS WEEK:

TRUST

Trust in the LORD with all your heart...-Proverbs 3:5

If your trust is great, then My generosity will be without limit.
–Jesus to Saint Faustina

THIS WEEK'S **SPECIFIC INTENTIONS** FOR MY CONFIRMAND(I):

Lord, I pray for these special intentions, and for my confirmand to always have a deep trust in the Lord, and I offer you this spiritual bouquet. Whatever life throws at him/her, allow him/her to trust in your plan and in your ability to care for him/her. By your grace, allow my confirmand to learn how to abandon oneself more fully to your will and not fear for the future. I pray that my confirmand may also trust in me as a sponsor to counsel, encourage, and be a model of firm trust and faith in God myself.

MY **SPIRITUAL BOUQUET** FOR THIS WEEK:

In the evening when you go to sleep,
hold your beads, doze off
reciting them, do like those babies who go
to sleep mumbling, "Mamma! Mamma!"

– *St. Bernadette*

CHARITY

So faith, hope, love abide, these three; but the greatest of these is love. –1 Corinthians 13:13

Charity is the form, mover, mother and root of all the virtues.
- Saint Thomas Aquinas

THIS WEEK'S **SPECIFIC INTENTIONS** FOR MY CONFIRMAND(I):

Lord, I pray for these special intentions, and for my confirmand to become a model of the virtue of charity. May he/she look to Your example, as well as the Blessed Mother and saints, who changed the world with their deep love. Allow love to radiate from him/her in a beautifully active way by his/her own free choices, bringing about powerful and transformative effects in his/her life and others. Help my confirmand always remember that hearts long for—and were made for—love: to love and to be loved, and that he/she can find the Source of Love in You, their Creator.

MY **SPIRITUAL BOUQUET** FOR THIS WEEK:

MEEKNESS

Put on then, as God's chosen ones, holy and beloved,
compassion, kindness, lowliness, meekness, and patience,
forbearing one another and, if one has a complaint against
another, forgiving each other; as the Lord has forgiven you, so you
also must forgive. –Colossians 3:12-13

Nothing is more powerful than meekness. For as fire is extinguished
by water, so a mind inflated by anger is subdued by meekness.
–St. John Chrysostom

THIS WEEK'S **SPECIFIC INTENTIONS** FOR MY CONFIRMAND(I):

Lord, I pray for these special intentions, and for my confirmand to
grow in meekness. With your grace, allow my confirmand to
become very good at moderating anger and controlling
resentment toward others, finding strength through submission to
God. I pray that in situations that provoke him/her to anger or un-
forgiveness, he/she instead keeps a sense of peace in adversity.

MY **SPIRITUAL BOUQUET** FOR THIS WEEK:

JOY

Clap your hands, all peoples! Shout to God with loud songs of joy!
–Psalm 47: 1

Joy is a net of love by which we catch souls.
- Saint Teresa of Calcutta

THIS WEEK'S **SPECIFIC INTENTIONS** FOR MY CONFIRMAND(I):

Lord, I pray for these special intentions, and for my confirmand to exhibit and possess great joy, and I offer you this spiritual bouquet. By your grace, may he/she always look for authentic, fulfilling happiness through relationship with you, rather than through money, possessions, fame, or other fleeting and earthly things. Fill him/her with joy to share with others, so he/she can become a light for you in our often-dark world.

MY **SPIRITUAL BOUQUET** FOR THIS WEEK:

WISDOM

To get wisdom is better than gold... - Proverbs 16:16

Dost thou hold wisdom to be anything other than truth,
wherein we behold and embrace the supreme good?
–St. Augustine

THIS WEEK'S **SPECIFIC INTENTIONS** FOR MY CONFIRMAND(I):

Lord, I pray for these special intentions, and for my confirmand to
possess the gift of wisdom, and I offer you this spiritual bouquet. By
your grace, allow him/her to grow in this highest gift of the Holy
Spirit, by which he/she will come to value the things we believe by
faith. Help my confirmand to have the wisdom to live a holy life
and value created things because of you who created them. I
pray he/she will share wisdom with others, too, so others may learn
and come to love the truth of the Christian faith as well.

MY **SPIRITUAL BOUQUET** FOR THIS WEEK:

FRIENDSHIP WITH THE SAINTS

And when he had taken the scroll, the four living creatures and the twenty-four elders fell down before the Lamb, each holding a harp, and with golden bowls full of incense, which are the prayers of the saints. –Revelation 5:8

Sanctity is beautiful! It is a beautiful way! The saints give us a message. They tell us: be faithful to the Lord, because the Lord does not disappoint! –Pope Francis

THIS WEEK'S **SPECIFIC INTENTIONS** FOR MY CONFIRMAND(I):

Lord, I pray for these special intentions, and for my confirmand to develop strong friendships with the saints. Give him/her a desire to learn more about the lives of the saints, to ask for their intercession, and to live in imitation of their holiness. May he/she acquire special patron saints along the Christian walk, who can inspire my confirmand to remain faithful to God and radically change the world around him/her with their love.

MY **SPIRITUAL BOUQUET** FOR THIS WEEK:

CLOSENESS WITH THE ANGELS

See that you do not despise one of these little ones; for I tell you that in heaven their angels always see the face of my Father who is in heaven. –Matthew 18:10

In this way is he [the true Christian] always pure for prayer. He also prays in the society of angels... he is never out of their holy keeping. –Clement of Alexandria

THIS WEEK'S **SPECIFIC INTENTIONS** FOR MY CONFIRMAND(I):

Lord, I pray for these special intentions, and for my confirmand to develop a closeness with God's angels. I pray that, in appropriate time, he/she may be aware of the spiritual battle between good and evil going on in our world, and call on the angels' help in spiritual combat. May my confirmand have a strong bond with his/her guardian angel in particular, who is tasked with guarding, protecting, ruling, and guiding him/her through this sometimes-messy life.

MY **SPIRITUAL BOUQUET** FOR THIS WEEK:

KNOWLEDGE

An intelligent mind acquires knowledge, and the ear of the wise seeks knowledge. - Proverbs 18:15

We can't have full knowledge all at once. We must start by believing; then afterwards we may be led on to master the evidence for ourselves. –Saint Thomas Aquinas

THIS WEEK'S **SPECIFIC INTENTIONS** FOR MY CONFIRMAND(I):

Lord, I pray for these special intentions, and for my confirmand to possess the gift of knowledge, and I offer you this spiritual bouquet. By your grace, allow him/her to have the ability to judge things according to the truths of the Catholic faith, and see circumstances in his/her life as you see them. With this knowledge, may he/she also recognize your purpose for his/her life.

MY **SPIRITUAL BOUQUET** FOR THIS WEEK:

KINDNESS

[A]s servants of God we commend ourselves in every way:… by purity, knowledge, forbearance, kindness, the Holy Spirit, genuine love… –2 Corinthians 6:4,6

Be the living expression of God's kindness—kindness in your face, kindness in your eyes, kindness in your smile, kindness in your warm greeting. –Saint Teresa of Calcutta

THIS WEEK'S **SPECIFIC INTENTIONS** FOR MY CONFIRMAND(I):

Lord, I pray for these special intentions, and for my confirmand to become a vessel of kindness, and I offer you this spiritual bouquet. By your grace, allow him/her to treat others as he/she would want to be treated (or better!) and always look for opportunities to extend a warm, loving, merciful and *kind* hand to anyone in need. I pray that my confirmand will be motivated to spread kindness at home and elsewhere in some small way, every day.

MY **SPIRITUAL BOUQUET** FOR THIS WEEK:

EVANGELIZATION

For if I preach the gospel, that gives me no ground for boasting.
For necessity is laid upon me. Woe to me if I do not preach the
gospel! –1 Corinthians 9:16

Every Christian is challenged, here and now, to be actively
engaged in evangelization; indeed, anyone who has truly
experienced God's saving love does not need much time or
lengthy training to go out and proclaim that love.
–Pope Francis

THIS WEEK'S **SPECIFIC INTENTIONS** FOR MY CONFIRMAND(I):

Lord, I pray for these special intentions, and for my confirmand to
be fervent in the mission of evangelization, in which we are all
called to participate at baptism. May he/she be filled with the joy
and love of Jesus and the Gospel, and then be fervent in sharing it
with others. I pray that my confirmand will always have the
courage and passion to share the faith with others, even when it's
difficult or unpopular to do so.

MY **SPIRITUAL BOUQUET** FOR THIS WEEK:

UNDERSTANDING

[W]e look not to the things that are seen but to the things that are unseen; for the things that are seen are transient, but the things that are unseen are eternal.
−2 Corinthians 4:18

Understanding is the reward of faith. Therefore, seek not to understand that you may believe, but believe that you may understand. −Saint Augustine

THIS WEEK'S **SPECIFIC INTENTIONS** FOR MY CONFIRMAND(I):

Lord, I pray for these special intentions, and for my confirmand to grow in understanding, and I offer you this spiritual bouquet. Allow him/her to grasp, in some incomplete but beautiful way, the essence of your truth and the truths of the Catholic faith, so he/she can possess an unwavering conviction about what he/she believes.

MY **SPIRITUAL BOUQUET** FOR THIS WEEK:

Prayer is the **best weapon**
we possess.
It is the **key** that opens the
heart of God.

-Saint Padre Pio

MODESTY

Do you not know that your body is a temple of the Holy Spirit within you, which you have from God? You are not your own; you were bought with a price. So glorify God in your body.
–1 Corinthians 6:19-20

Let your modesty be a sufficient incitement, yea, an exhortation to everyone to be at peace on their merely looking at you.
–Saint Ignatius of Loyola

THIS WEEK'S **SPECIFIC INTENTIONS** FOR MY CONFIRMAND(I):

Lord, I pray for these special intentions, and for my confirmand to be modest in thought, word, and dress, and I present to you this spiritual bouquet. By your grace, allow him/her to see and embrace modesty as a practice that upholds one's spiritual dignity as your son or daughter. Help increase in him/her a deep respect for the human person, so modesty becomes a natural corollary of that respect.

MY **SPIRITUAL BOUQUET** FOR THIS WEEK:

EMPATHY

Rejoice with those who rejoice, weep with those who weep.
–Romans 12:15

There are two forms of intelligence. One is of the mind, the other of the heart. In the moral sphere there can be no doubt that the empathy of the heart is incomparably more important than the photography of the mind. Through the mind we can know and understand, but through the heart we can love, serve, and change the world.
–Dr. Donald DeMarco

THIS WEEK'S **SPECIFIC INTENTIONS** FOR MY CONFIRMAND(I):

Lord, I pray for these special intentions, and for my confirmand to possess great empathy. By your grace, allow him/her to enter into other people's feelings, needs, and sufferings. Our world—and our home—is full of souls in need of empathy. Help my confirmand fill that need.

MY **SPIRITUAL BOUQUET** FOR THIS WEEK:

SELF-CONTROL

He who keeps his mouth and his tongue keeps himself out of trouble. - Proverbs 21:23

Look toward Heaven, where Jesus Christ is waiting for you with His saints! Be faithful in his love, and fight courageously for your souls.
–Saint Felicity

THIS WEEK'S **SPECIFIC INTENTIONS** FOR MY CONFIRMAND(I):

Lord, I pray for these special intentions, and for my confirmand to grow in self-control. Help my confirmand overcome temptation and deny him/herself things that could draw him/her away from you. Allow my confirmand to guard his/her words, which are often used without discretion, and to monitor thoughts and actions, which, when uncontrolled, could harm oneself or others.

MY **SPIRITUAL BOUQUET** FOR THIS WEEK:

WORK & LEISURE

Commit your work to the LORD, and your plans will be established.
-Proverbs 16:3

Leisure is only possible when we are at one with ourselves. We tend to overwork as a means of self-escape, as a way of trying to justify our existence. –Josef Pieper

THIS WEEK'S **SPECIFIC INTENTIONS** FOR MY CONFIRMAND(I):

Lord, I pray for these special intentions, and for my confirmand to have a healthy and fulfilling relationship with both work and leisure. Whether it be work at school, in the home, or in a professional environment, allow my confirmand to offer labor to you, Lord, seeing the good that comes from meaningful work. By your grace, also help him/her to be restful and embrace leisure, avoiding the "workaholism" prevalent in our day so as to maximize time spent with loved ones, doing the things he/she loves.

MY **SPIRITUAL BOUQUET** FOR THIS WEEK:

PIETY

Not every one who says to me, `Lord, Lord,' shall enter the kingdom of heaven, but he who does the will of my Father who is in heaven. –Matthew 7:21

[Piety] indicates our belonging to God, our deep bond with him, a relationship that gives meaning to our whole life and keeps us resolute, in communion with him, even during the most difficult and troubled moments. –Pope Francis

THIS WEEK'S **SPECIFIC INTENTIONS** FOR MY CONFIRMAND(I):

Lord, I pray for these special intentions, and for my confirmand to grow in piety, and I offer you this spiritual bouquet. By your grace, instill in him/her a burning desire to worship you and to serve you with one's whole self and life. I pray that this worship and service stem not merely from a sense of duty, but because of their immense love for you.

MY **SPIRITUAL BOUQUET** FOR THIS WEEK:

FORGIVENESS

Then Peter came up and said to him, "Lord, how often shall my brother sin against me, and I forgive him? As many as seven times?" Jesus said to him, "I do not say to you seven times, but seventy times seven." –Matthew 18:21-22

He who knows how to forgive prepares for himself many graces from God. As often as I look upon the cross, so often will I forgive with all my heart. -St. Faustina

THIS WEEK'S **SPECIFIC INTENTIONS** FOR MY CONFIRMAND(I):

Lord, I pray for these special intentions, and for my confirmand to learn to forgive well and often, and I offer you this spiritual bouquet. By your grace, help him/her learn to extend forgiveness when it is uncomfortable or when it seems impossible, recognizing the ultimate example of forgiveness you have provided for us, when even on the cross you forgave your enemies who put you to death.

MY **SPIRITUAL BOUQUET** FOR THIS WEEK:

HEALTH & SAFETY

>>)———(((

Beloved, I pray that all may go well with you and that you may be
in health; I know that it is well with your soul.
–3 John 1:2

THIS WEEK'S **SPECIFIC INTENTIONS** FOR MY CONFIRMAND(I):

Lord, I pray for these special intentions, and for my confirmand's
health and safety. God, this world can be scary and cruel, and
sometimes innocent young souls experience violence and pain
that we can only pray they might never endure. I ask that, through
your mercy, you protect them from serious illness and harm. Should
he/she experience pain or be in a dangerous situation, send your
host of angels to be with him/her, and give my confirmand the
grace to endure anything he/she may battle. Finally, when I am
tempted to be fearful or let my imagination run wild, whisper in my
heart a reminder to trust in you, knowing you love my confirmand
even more.

MY **SPIRITUAL BOUQUET** FOR THIS WEEK:

Virtues are formed by prayer.
Prayer preserves temperance. Prayer
suppresses anger.
Prayer prevents emotions of pride and
envy.
Prayer draws into the soul
the Holy Spirit,
and raises man to Heaven.

- St. Ephraem of Syria

FEAR OF THE LORD

Fear God, and keep his commandments; for this is the whole duty of man. –Ecclesiastes 12:13

For the absence of the fear of God is arrogance and pride. How dare sinners sashay up to God as a chum without first falling down in repentance and fear and calling on the Blood of Christ to save us? –Dr. Peter Kreeft

THIS WEEK'S **SPECIFIC INTENTIONS** FOR MY CONFIRMAND(I):

Lord, I pray for these special intentions, and for my confirmand to grow in the Holy Spirit's gift of fear of the Lord, and I offer you this spiritual bouquet. By your grace, instill in him/her a desire never to offend you, either in word or deed, my God, and the confidence that you will give him/her the grace to make this possible. Fill my confirmand with awe and wonder of you, so as to respect you out of deep love.

MY **SPIRITUAL BOUQUET** FOR THIS WEEK:

GENTLENESS

But the wisdom from above is first pure, then peaceable, gentle, open to reason, full of mercy and good fruits, without uncertainty or insincerity. –James 3:17

Nothing is so strong as gentleness, nothing so gentle as real strength. –Saint Francis de Sales

THIS WEEK'S **SPECIFIC INTENTIONS** FOR MY CONFIRMAND(I):

Lord, I pray for these special intentions, and for my confirmand to grow in gentleness, and I offer you this spiritual bouquet. By your grace and through my teaching, allow my confirmand to learn how to act calmly and politely toward others. I pray that others may characterize him/her by humility and thankfulness toward you. I also ask, Lord, that you give my confirmand the strength to correct and accept corrections *gently*, humbly, and lovingly.

MY **SPIRITUAL BOUQUET** FOR THIS WEEK:

RELATIONSHIP WITH FRIENDS

There are friends who pretend to be friends, but there is a friend who sticks closer than a brother.
–Proverbs 18:24

There is nothing on this earth more to be prized than true friendship. –Saint Thomas Aquinas

THIS WEEK'S **SPECIFIC INTENTIONS** FOR MY CONFIRMAND(I):

Lord, I pray for these special intentions, and for my confirmand to have strong, *good* friendships. I know the impact that friends can have on my confirmand. A good friend can lead him/her toward a life of virtue, and a bad friend can lead him/her down paths of vice. By your grace, lead my confirmand toward friends with good character, who encourage him/her to be more like the person you desire my confirmand to be. Also, I pray that my confirmand always *be* a good friend to others, so friends may see in him/her a reflection of you.

MY **SPIRITUAL BOUQUET** FOR THIS WEEK:

COUNSEL

The wisdom of a prudent man is to discern his way, but the folly of fools is deceiving. –Proverbs 14:8

Nothing is so strong as gentleness, nothing so gentle as real strength. –Saint Francis de Sales

THIS WEEK'S **SPECIFIC INTENTIONS** FOR MY CONFIRMAND(I):

Lord, I pray for these special intentions, and for my confirmand to possess the Holy Spirit's gift of counsel, and I offer you this spiritual bouquet. By your grace, help my confirmand learn to judge how best to act in any situation, calling on the Holy Spirit's guidance. I pray he/she will defend the truths of the faith, always living according to them as a faithful disciple of yours. May his/her good counsel serve also as a witness to others, so he/she may inspire friends to also act prudently.

MY **SPIRITUAL BOUQUET** FOR THIS WEEK:

SOLICITUDE

Love one another with brotherly affection; outdo one another in showing honor. –Romans 12:10

What is the mark of love for your neighbor? Not to seek what is for your own benefit, but what is for the benefit of the one loved, both in body and in soul. –St. Basil

THIS WEEK'S **SPECIFIC INTENTIONS** FOR MY CONFIRMAND(I):

Lord, I pray for these special intentions, and for my confirmand to grow in solicitude, and I offer you this spiritual bouquet. By your grace, help him/her exhibit great "brotherly love," by demonstrating care and concern for the wellbeing of those around him/her. Rather than being envious, I pray my confirmand will admire the skills and accomplishments of others, and excel at congratulating and encouraging the people you place in his/her path.

MY **SPIRITUAL BOUQUET** FOR THIS WEEK:

INDEPENDENCE

[A]nd I shall walk at liberty, for I have sought thy precepts.
–Psalm 119:45

Freedom consists not in doing what we like, but in having the right
to do what we ought. –Pope Saint John Paul II

THIS WEEK'S **SPECIFIC INTENTIONS** FOR MY CONFIRMAND(I):

Lord, I pray for these special intentions, and for my confirmand to become strong, independent adults. By your grace, allow my confirmand to learn how to exercise his/her own freedom and independence, at the appropriate times as he/she grows up, and then bestow him/her with the ability to make good decisions to care for oneself, exercising the freedom to choose what is right. I pray that my confirmand may always maintain a healthy relationship with authority, compatible with his/her mature freedom.

MY **SPIRITUAL BOUQUET** FOR THIS WEEK:

GOODNESS

Surely goodness and mercy shall follow me all the days of my life;
and I shall dwell in the house of the LORD forever.
–Psalm 23:6

A morally good act requires the goodness of its object, of its end,
and of its circumstances together.
–Catechism of the Catholic Church 1760

THIS WEEK'S **SPECIFIC INTENTIONS** FOR MY CONFIRMAND(I):

Lord, I pray for these special intentions, and for my confirmand to possess the Holy Spirit's fruit of goodness, and I offer you this spiritual bouquet. By your grace, Lord, allow my confirmand to honor you by doing what is right. Help him/her to avoid sin and make morally good choices, a demonstration of love for you and a response of gratitude for *your* great goodness toward us.

MY **SPIRITUAL BOUQUET** FOR THIS WEEK:

Without prayer nothing good is done.
God's works are done
with our hands joined,
and on our knees. Even when we run,
we must remain spiritually
kneeling before Him.

-Blessed Luigi Orione

SELF-AWARENESS

Examine yourselves, to see whether you are holding to your faith.
Test yourselves. Do you not realize that Jesus Christ is in you? -
unless indeed you fail to meet the test!
–2 Corinthians 13:5

Know thyself, and thy faults, and thus live." —St. Augustine

THIS WEEK'S **SPECIFIC INTENTIONS** FOR MY CONFIRMAND(I):

Lord, I pray for these special intentions, and for my confirmand to
exhibit great self-awareness. By your grace, Lord, I pray he/she will
always aspire to self-improvement, being aware of his/her faults
and actively seeking to uproot them and grow in holiness.
Enlighten him/her to recognize when he/she is far from you. Help
my confirmand to be aware of his/her virtues and talents, rejoicing
in them as gifts from you, exercising them for your glory.

MY **SPIRITUAL BOUQUET** FOR THIS WEEK:

RESPECT FOR LIFE

You shall not kill. –Exodus 20:13

"Before I formed you in the womb I knew you, and before you were born I consecrated you... --Jeremiah 1:5

The fundamental human right, the presupposition of every other right, is the right to life itself...from the moment of conception until its natural end. –Pope Benedict XVI

THIS WEEK'S **SPECIFIC INTENTIONS** FOR MY CONFIRMAND(I):

Lord, I pray for these special intentions, and for my confirmand to always have a deep respect for life. By his/her words and actions, Lord, help my confirmand be passionately pro-life, believing in the sanctity of all human life from conception to natural death, and be open to life in his/her own future family. Inspire him/her to defend life issues at home and publically, even when it is unpopular to do so.

MY **SPIRITUAL BOUQUET** FOR THIS WEEK:

MEANINGFUL SUFFERING

I consider that the sufferings of this present time are not worth
comparing with the glory that is to be revealed to us.
–Romans 8:18

If God sends you many sufferings, it is a sign that He has great
plans for you and certainly wants to make you a saint.
-St. Ignatius Loyola

THIS WEEK'S **SPECIFIC INTENTIONS** FOR MY CONFIRMAND(I):

Lord, I pray for these special intentions, and for my confirmand to
suffer with dignity. Though it may break my heart to see my
confirmand suffer, I ask that when he/she does, you infuse him/her
with grace in moments of suffering, allowing my confirmand to see
the redemptive power in suffering. I pray that my confirmand will
offer up pain and unite sufferings with yours on the cross, never
thinking that suffering is meaningless.

MY **SPIRITUAL BOUQUET** FOR THIS WEEK:

SANCTITY

You, therefore, must be perfect, as your heavenly Father is perfect.
–Matthew 5:48

Life holds only one tragedy: not to have been a saint.
–Léon Bloy

THIS WEEK'S **SPECIFIC INTENTIONS** FOR MY CONFIRMAND(I):

Lord, I pray for these special intentions, and for my confirmand to be a saint in heaven someday, and I offer you this spiritual bouquet. More than any other prayer intention, Lord, I implore you to mold my confirmand into a great saint. May he/she come to see that you are calling him/her to the heights of holiness, no matter what state or vocation in life my confirmand may find him/herself. Help my confirmand to see small ways to grow in sanctity every day and be fervent in taking those little steps to draw closer to you and become more like you, so he/she may spend eternity with you in the company of your saints.

MY **SPIRITUAL BOUQUET** FOR THIS WEEK:

In the family of prayer,
in strong moments and in difficult periods,
may we be entrusted to one another,
in order that every one of us in the family may be
protected by God's love.

-Pope Francis-

Thank you, sponsors, for joining me on this special prayer journey for your confirmand. May you always turn to prayer as the source of healing for your confirmand's past, a wellspring of grace for their present, and a fountain of hope for their future.

I would be immensely grateful if you would recommend this prayer journal to others, including the ministries at your parish and diocese. Please share your feedback with me, too, or contact me for bulk discount quotes on this journal and others at:

CatholicKatieOnline@gmail.com

You can also find me and other great resources to raise faith-filled families at **KatieWarner.com,** on Facebook at Facebook.com/ CatholicKatieOnline, and on Instagram @katiewarnercatholic.

AMDG!

KATIE

OTHER BOOKS BY KATIE WARNER

LEARN MORE AT KATIEWARNER.COM/SHOP

Made in the USA
Coppell, TX
27 October 2020